Cricket

Written by
Jill Atkins

Ransom

This man is playing cricket.
He is a batsman.
He has pads and gloves.
He has a cricket bat.

This man is playing cricket.
He is a wicket keeper.
He has pads and gloves, too.
He is behind the stumps.

This man is playing cricket.
He is a bowler.
He has a cricket ball.
The ball is red.

This man is playing cricket.
He is a fielder.
He will stop the ball.

This man is playing cricket.
He runs in and bowls the ball.

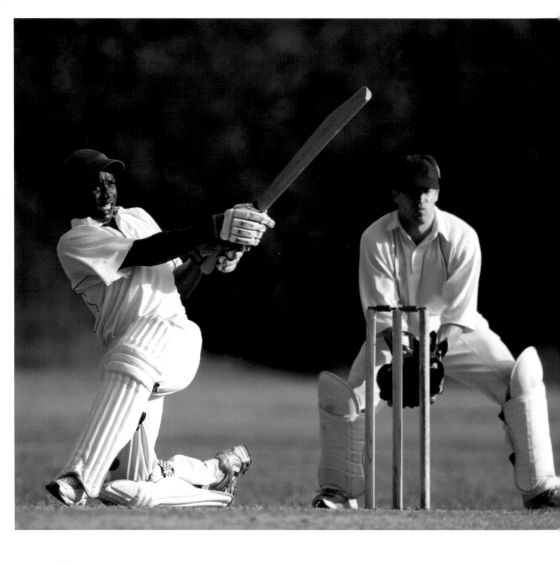

This man is playing cricket.
He hits the ball.
The ball is up in the air.

Oh no!
This man will catch the ball.

The batsman is out!